A Single Man's Guide to Easy Meals

George F. Simon

authorHOUSE™

1663 LIBERTY DRIVE, SUITE 200
BLOOMINGTON, INDIANA 47403
(800) 839-8640
WWW.AUTHORHOUSE.COM

First published by AuthorHouse 11/08/05

ISBN: 1-4208-7556-6 (sc)

Library of Congress Control Number: 2005907370

Printed in the United States of America
Bloomington, Indiana

This book is printed on acid-free paper.

In Gratitude

To my wife Mary Ann who always supports me and two great ladies in Texas, Shay and Nancy, who encouraged me to put this book together. I told you I'd remember !

Forward

Not long ago I was given a job opportunity that I could not pass up. I packed and moved by myself to Dallas, Texas. So, at the age of 54, having been married almost 30 years, I found myself alone in Dallas some 1100 miles from my wife. Now that was bad enough but I quickly realized that I don't really know how to cook, except for some barbecuing. After working 10 to 12 hours a day I didn't want to cook and I didn't want to end the day cleaning several pots and pans and the associated cooking utensils. I began looking for recipes that required a bare minimum of cooking pots and pans, where the meal could be cooked in one container and in less than one hour. My wife sent me all the recipes she had, and co-workers gave me some.

I realized that I could not be the only male in this situation and so decided to put together this recipe book dedicated especially to single men everywhere. All of the recipes in this book can be made usually in one cooking utensil, and can be made in less than one hour. I have made each recipe and if I can make it, anyone can. I especially enjoyed the last chapter entitled "Things That Go With Beer." You select the brand of beer.

I hope you enjoy the recipes as much as I do. Finally, a recipe book for men everywhere!

Contents

Chicken Recipes

Chicken and Noodles Casserole

One 10 ¾ ounce can condensed cream of
   chicken soup
½ cup milk
1/3 cup grated Parmesan cheese
3 cups (dry measure) medium egg noodles
2 cups cooked chicken (Swanson's canned
   chicken or 2 cooked chicken breasts cubed)

Cook the noodles, drain, and set aside.
Combine in 3 quart sauce pan soup, milk cheese and salt
and pepper to taste. Add noodles and chicken, and heat
over medium heat.

Makes 4 servings   30 minutes

Shopping List

Chicken and Noodles Casserole

1 can of chicken soup
1 bag of grated Parmesan cheese
1 bag of medium egg noodles
2 chicken breasts (pre-cooked)

Chicken and Potatoes

4 chicken breasts
1 ½ cups of chopped onions
3 diced medium potatoes
1 can cream of chicken soup
1 can cream of celery soup
1 cup peas and carrots

Combine all ingredients in baking dish, salt and pepper to taste. Bake in oven at 375 for 40 minutes.

Serves 4

Shopping List

Chicken and Potatoes

4 chicken breasts
1 large yellow onion
1 bag potatoes
1 can cream of chicken soup
1 can of cream of celery soup
1 bag of frozen peas & carrots

Creamy Chicken and Broccoli

4 Boneless chicken breasts cubed
1 package (10oz.) chopped drained broccoli
1 ½ cups milk
1 ½ cups uncooked Minute Rice
½ lb. Velveeta cheese cubed
½ cup mayonnaise
½ cup sour cream

Pre heat oven to 375, mix all ingredients and spoon into a 12x8 inch baking dish. Bake 35 minutes. Sprinkle top with shredded cheese, if desired, after 30 minutes of baking time.

Serves 6

Shopping List

Creamy Chicken and Broccoli

4 boneless chicken breasts
1 package of frozen broccoli pieces
Milk
1 box Minute Rice
1 block of Velveeta cheese
1 small container sour cream
1 jar of mayonnaise

Chicken Noodle Casserole

1 Package (8-ounce) medium noodles, cooked
  and drained
2 cups diced cooked chicken (Swanson's canned
  chicken)
¼ cup diced green pepper
1 cup celery
2 cups evaporated milk
1 can of cream of chicken soup
½ teaspoon salt
1 ½ cups shredded sharp cheddar cheese

Place noodles in 2-quart casserole. In separate pan, stir
in chicken, pepper, celery, milk soup and salt. Heat on
medium heat. Stir until well blended. Pour mixture over
noodles and add cheese. Bake for 25 to 30 minutes at
375 or until cheese is bubbly.

Serves 5 to 6

Shopping List

Chicken Noodle Casserole

1 package medium noodles
1 package of Swanson's chicken
1 green pepper
1 stalk of celery
1 can of evaporated milk
1 can of cream of chicken soup
1 bag of shredded cheddar cheese

Creamy Chicken Vegetables

4 skinless boneless chicken breasts
1/8 tsp. garlic powder
¾ bag of noodles, cooked
1 can cream of mushroom soup
½ cup of milk
1 bag thawed and drained vegetable
    combination

Sprinkle chicken with garlic powder (salt to taste). Spray large skillet with cooking spray and heat at medium high. Brown breasts for 10 minutes or until browned on both sides. Set chicken aside. Add all other ingredients, heating to a boil. Add chicken and cover on low heat for 15 minutes. Serve over noodles.

Serves 4   40 minutes

Shopping List

Creamy Chicken Vegetables

4 skinless boneless chicken breasts
1 garlic powder
1 bag noodles
1 can of cream of mushroom soup
Milk
1 bag of frozen vegetables

Chicken and Stuffing Bake

4 cups herb stuffing
6 skinless chicken breast halves
1 can cream of mushroom soup
½ cup of milk
1 cup water
1 tbsp. margarine

Mix stuffing in bowl with 1 cup boiling water and margarine. Spoon stuffing across center of 3 quart baking dish and place chicken breasts on each side of stuffing. Mix soup and milk and pour over chicken. Bake at 400 for 15 to 20 minutes.

Serves 6

Shopping List

Chicken and Stuffing Bake

1 box herb stuffing
6 skinless chicken breasts
1 can of cream of mushroom soup
Milk
1 box Margarine

Chicken Fajita Pizzas

4 (6inch) flour tortillas
2 cups shredded cheddar cheese
1 cup (2 boneless chicken breasts Pre-cooked)
   Shredded
½ cup salsa
½ cup chopped green pepper
½ cup diced tomato
¼ cup pitted ripe olives

Preheat oven to 350. Place tortillas on cookie sheet and sprinkle with 2 tablespoons shredded cheese on each tortilla. Bake 3-4 minutes until cheese is melted. Mix chicken and salsa and spread on tortillas. Top with remaining cheese and bake 10 minutes. Top with remaining ingredients. Add sour cream to taste.

Serves 2   25 minutes

Shopping List

Chicken Fajita Pizza

1 package of flour tortillas
1 package of shredded cheddar cheese
2 boneless chicken breasts
1 jar salsa
1 green pepper
1 tomato
1 jar of ripe (black) olives

Picante Chicken Tacos

1 Tbsp. vegetable oil
1 lb. Boneless chicken breasts cut into thin
   strips
1 jar (16 oz.) thick and chunky Picante sauce
1 box soft taco shells
1 cup shredded lettuce
4 oz. Shredded cheese
½ cup sour cream

Heat oil in large skillet on high heat until hot. Add chicken and cook until no longer pink. Stir in Picante sauce and reduce heat to medium. Simmer 10 minutes stirring occasionally. Heat soft tacos in oven for 3 minutes at 300 or microwave for 15 seconds on high. Fill each shell with chicken Picante mixture and top with remaining ingredients.

Makes 12 tacos   25 minutes.

Shopping List

Picante Chicken Tacos

1 container vegetable oil
4 boneless skinless chicken breasts
1 jar of thick and chunky Picante salsa
1-box soft taco shells
1 head or 1 package of lettuce
1 package of shredded cheddar cheese
1 container sour cream

Lattice Top Chicken

1 can cream of chicken soup

1 cup milk

2 cups chopped cut chicken cooked

1 lb frozen vegetables

1 can Durkee's onions

1 cup Bisquick

1 egg

1 cup shredded cheese

Combine soup, ¾ cup milk, chicken, vegetables, 1/2 cup cheese and ½ can onions. Spread mixture in 8x12 greased (use margarine to grease dish) and bake at 425 for 10 minutes. Combine Bisquick, egg and milk, mix well and scoop in lattice design over chicken mixture. Bake at 425 for 25 minutes Put remaining cheese and onions on top of mixture the last 3 minutes.

Serves 6   45 minutes

Shopping List

Lattice Top Chicken

2 packages of Swanson's cooked chicken
1 can cream of chicken soup
Milk
1 package of frozen mixed vegetables
1 can of Durkee's onions
1 box of Bisquick
Eggs
1 package of shredded cheddar cheese

Chicken Pot Pie

2 cans Cream of
  Broccoli soup
1 cup milk
¼ tsp. Pepper
¼ cup chopped
  onions

4 cups combination
  vegetables
2 cups cooked chicken
1 can flaky biscuits
¼ tsp. Garlic salt

Combine all ingredients except the biscuits in an 8x12 baking dish and cook at 400 for 15 minutes. Cut the biscuits into quarters. Remove the dish from the oven and stir. Arrange biscuits over the chicken mixture and bake15 minutes or until the biscuits are golden brown.

Serves 5   40 minutes.

Shopping List

Chicken Pot Pie

2 cans of cream of Broccoli soup
Milk
1 medium yellow onion
1 bag of mixed vegetables
2 packages of Swanson's cooked chicken
1 can flaky biscuits
Garlic salt

Chicken and Broccoli Alfredo

½ cup milk
½ box of fettuccini noodles cooked and drained
1 lb. boneless chicken breasts cubed
1 pkg. Alfredo mix (McCormick's)
½ cup grated Parmesan cheese

Cook fettuccini according to directions. Add the broccoli the last 4 minutes of cooking time. Melt the butter in a skillet and cook the chicken until browned on both sides. Add Alfredo mix and follow directions. Add all ingredients to the noodles and mix thoroughly. Sprinkle with more Parmesan cheese if desired.

Serves 4   30 minutes

Shopping List

Chicken And Broccoli Alfredo

Milk
1 box fettuccini noodles
2 boneless chicken breasts
1 package of Alfredo mix (McCormick's)
1 can of grated Parmesan cheese

Chicken and Shrimp Alfredo

½ box Alfredo noodles cooked and drained
1 lb. cooked cubed chicken breast
¼ cup chopped green, and red pepper
½ lb. Pre-cooked and peeled shrimp
1 jar Alfredo sauce
2 tbsp butter

Preheat oven to 350. Cook and drain the noodles according to box directions. Add the chicken and shrimp and pepper to 2 qt. casserole along with the jar of Alfredo sauce and mix well. Bake for 25 minutes

Serves 4   30 minutes

Shopping List

Chicken and Shrimp Alfredo

1 box Alfredo noodles
3 boneless chicken breasts
1 each green and red pepper
1 bag frozen cooked and peeled shrimp
1 jar Alfredo sauce
1 package of butter

Chicken Cordon Bleu Casserole

20 oz. Cut broccoli (frozen)

2-2 ½ oz. Budig smoked chicken

1 lg. Can creamy mushroom soup

8 slices of Rye bread

12 oz. Cooked ham

1 package of shredded Swiss cheese

Line a 9x13-cooking pan with rye bread. Top with chicken, ham and broccoli. Pour soup over all and sprinkle with cheese. Bake in 350 oven for 30 minutes.

Serves 4   40 minutes

Shopping List

Chicken Cordon Bleu Casserole

1 package of frozen broccoli pieces
1 package of Budig smoked chicken
1 can of cream of mushroom soup
1 loaf of rye bread
1 package cooked ham
1 package of Swiss cheese

Beef Recipes

Ground Beef Penne Pasta Bake

12 oz. Penne pasta

1 cup chopped onion

1 can Italian style
tomato sauce

1 can tomato paste
with roasted
garlic

4 cups shredded
Mozzarella
cheese.

1 lb. Ground beef

1 small can mushrooms

1 can diced tomatoes
with herbs

½ cup green pepper

Cook pasta according to package directions and drain. At the same time cook ground beef and onions in large skillet over medium heat for 5 minutes and drain. Add the tomato sauce, undrained tomatoes, tomatoes, tomato paste, green pepper and ½ cup water stirring occasionally for 10 minutes. Layer ½ of pasta, sauce and cheese in a 13x9 baking dish and repeat. Cover and bake in preheated 350 oven for 20 minutes.

Serves 6   40 minutes

Shopping List

Ground Beef Penne Pasta Bake

1 package of Penne pasta
2 medium yellow onions
1 can of tomato sauce (Italian style)
1 can of tomato paste with roasted garlic
1 bag of shredded Mozzarella cheese
1lb. Ground beef
1 can of mushrooms
1 can of diced tomatoes with herbs
1 green pepper

Spaghetti Pie

½ lb. Ground beef   ¼ tsp. Basil

½ box spaghetti   ¼ tsp. Oregano

1 egg (beaten)   ¼ tsp. Rosemary

1 tbsp. Margarine   ½ tsp. Garlic powder

1/3 cup parmesan   1 15 oz. Jar of tomato
   cheese   sauce

Cook spaghetti and drain, in large skillet cook ground beef and drain. Add beaten egg, melted margarine, cheese and herbs to spaghetti and mix well. Press spaghetti in a pie pan and add the ground beef and then the tomato sauce. Top with cheese and bake in 350 degree oven for 25 minutes. Allow to stand 10 minutes before cutting.

Serves 4   45 minutes

Shopping List

Spaghetti Pie

½ lb. Ground beef
1 box spaghetti
Eggs
1 package of Margarine
1 can of Parmesan cheese
1 small jar of Basil, Oregano, Rosemary and
Garlic powder
1, 15 oz. Jar of tomato sauce

Sloppy Joes

1 lb. Hamburger	2 tbsp. Mustard
1 medium chopped onion	1 tbsp. Worcestershire sauce
2 tbsp sugar	½ cup catsup
1 tbsp vinegar	½ cup finely chopped green pepper

Brown ground beef in skillet along with onion and green pepper. Drain ground beef mixture. Mix other ingredients in bowl. Add the other ingredients to beef and mix well. Simmer 15 to 20 minutes.

Serves 5   30 minutes

Shopping List

Sloppy Joes

1 lb. Ground meet
1 medium yellow onion
Sugar
1 bottle dark vinegar
1 jar of yellow mustard
1 bottle of Worcestershire sauce
1 bottle catsup
1 green pepper

German Spaghetti

2 lbs. Ground beef
1 lb. Bacon
1 lb. Spaghetti cooked
1 26 oz. Can of tomato
    soup

1 cup diced celery
1 onion chopped
1 diced green pepper

Brown beef in a skillet, drain and pour into a large baking dish. Cut bacon into small pieces and fry 4 – 5 minutes; add onion, pepper and celery and continue to cook until bacon is almost crisp and vegetables are tender. Drain grease from skillet and add to ground beef. Mix in spaghetti and tomato soup until well blended. Cover and bake in 350 degree oven for 30 minutes.

Serves 6   40 minutes

Shopping List

German Spaghetti

2 lbs. Ground beef
1 lb. Bacon
1 bag of spaghetti
1 can of tomato soup
1 stalk of celery
1 yellow onion
1 green pepper

Cheeseburger Pie

1 lb. Ground beef   1 cup chopped onion
½ tsp. Salt   1 cup shredded cheddar
                         cheese
1 cup milk   ½ cup Bisquick
2 eggs

Cook ground beef in large skillet on medium heat. While beef is pink add onion. Once cooked, drain and add salt. Spread in a 9" pie pan and sprinkle with cheese. Mix eggs Bisquick and milk, add to the pie and stir into the mixture. Bake for 25 minutes in a 400 degree oven.

Serves 6   35 minutes

Shopping List

Cheeseburger Pie

1 lb. ground beef
Salt
Milk
Eggs
1 yellow onion
1 bag of shredded cheddar cheese
1 box of Bisquick

Weekday Casserole

1 lb. Bacon, diced

1 small onion
diced

1 can tomato soup

1 can peas

1 ½ cups shredded
cheddar cheese

1 lb ground beef

10 oz medium noodles
cooked

1 can mushroom soup

½ cup water

Preheat oven to 325. Cook noodles and drain. Fry bacon, ground beef and onion until browned. Drain excess fat. Mix drained noodles with beef mixture, add peas, soup and water. Place in large casserole dish and top with cracker crumbs that were lightly sautéed in melted butter and sprinkle cheese over all. Bake for 35 minutes at 325.

Serves 5   40 minutes

Shopping List

Weekday Casserole

1 package of bacon
1 yellow onion
1 can of tomato soup
1 can of peas
1 bag of shredded cheddar cheese
1 lb. ground beef
1 bag of noodles
1 can of mushroom soup

Joe's Favorite

1 lb. ground beef	1 tbsp. Corn starch
1 small chopped onion	¼ cup water
1 can beef broth	1 box potato flakes
1 can or ½ bag frozen corn	

In a large skillet, brown beef and onion. Drain excess fat. Add beef broth. Combine water and corn starch and mix well to eliminate lumps. Add to meat mixture stirring constantly over low heat until thickened. Make potatoes according to box directions. Serve the ground beef and gravy over mashed potatoes, add corn to the top.

Serves 6   35 minutes

Shopping List

Joe's Favorite

1 lb. ground beef
1 yellow onion
1 can beef broth
1 box cornstarch
1 box instant potatoes
1 box frozen corn

Mom's Coming! Casserole

1 package (8oz.) wide noodles

½ cup chopped onion

1 cup creamed cottage cheese

1 8oz. Package cream cheese

½ cup sour cream

1 lb. ground beef

¼ cup chopped green pepper

1 can (28oz.) tomato sauce

Cook noodles and drain. Brown beef and drain. Stir in tomato sauce and remove from heat. Combine cottage cheese, cream cheese, sour cream pepper and onions. Spread ½ of cooked noodles in a greased 2 qt. Casserole. Cover with cheese mixture then add remaining noodles. Spread the meat mixture over the top and bake at 350 for 30 minutes.

Serves 6   40 minutes

Shopping List

Mom's Coming Casserole

1 package wide noodles
1 container creamed cottage cheese
1package sour cream
1 green pepper
1 yellow onion
1 8oz. Package cream cheese
1 lb. ground cheese
1 can (28oz.) tomato sauce

Beef and Cheddar Casserole

1 lb. ground beef

1/3 cup chopped
   onion

1/3 cup water

1 can cheddar
   cheese soup

1 cup chopped tomatoes

1 tsp. Mustard

1 can whole kernel corn

2 cups cooked drained
   noodles

Brown beef and onion on medium heat and drain fat. Add water, soup, tomatoes, mustard, corn and noodles. Mix well and pour into a 2 qt. Casserole and bake at 350 for 30 minutes.

Serves 5   40 minutes

Shopping List

Beef and Cheddar Casserole

1 lb. ground beef
1 yellow onion
1 can cheddar cheese soup
1 can of chopped tomatoes
1 jar of mustard
1 can whole kernel corn
1 bag noodles

Burger Bake

1 ¼ lbs. Ground beef	½ cup sour cream
½ cup chopped onion	1 egg beaten
1 8oz. Tomato sauce	¼ cup chopped green pepper
1 ½ cups shredded Monterey Jack cheese	½ tsp garlic salt
2 tsp. Chili powder	1 can biscuits

Brown beef, onion and pepper and drain. Stir in tomato sauce, chili powder and garlic salt. Simmer for 5 minutes. Combine ½ cup shredded cheese, sour cream and egg. Remove meat from heat and stir in the sour cream. Separate biscuits from can and cut in half. Put 10 halves over the bottom of 9x9 ungreased baking pan. Spoon meat over biscuit dough and then arrange the remaining 10 half biscuits on top of meat mixture and sprinkle with remaining cheese. Bake for 25 minutes at 375.

Serves 5   35 minutes

Shopping List

Burger Bake

1 ¼ lb. ground beef
1 yellow onion
1 8oz. can tomato sauce
1 bag shredded Monterey Jack cheese
1 jar chili powder
1 container sour cream
Eggs
1 green pepper
Salt
1 can biscuits

Fall Vegetable Beef Casserole

1 package mixed
   vegetables in
   butter sauce

1 ½ cups wide
   noodles

1 lb. ground beef

1 cup sliced celery

½ cup chopped onion

½ cup catsup

1 14 oz can tomatoes,
   diced

1 4oz. Can mushrooms

¼ tsp. Pepper

1 tsp. Salt

Prepare vegetables according to package directions. Drain cooked noodles and mushrooms. Brown beef, onions and celery in skillet. Drain off fat and add noodles, catsup, vegetables, tomatoes, mushrooms pepper and salt. Cover and simmer 30-40 minutes.

Serves 5

Shopping List

Fall Vegetable Beef Casserole

1 package mixed vegetables in butter sauce
1 bag wide noodles
1 lb. ground beef
1 stalk celery
1 yellow onion
1 bottle catsup
1 14 oz. can diced tomatoes
1 can mushrooms
Pepper
Salt

Macaroni Beef Casserole

1 lb. ground beef

1 large onion chopped

2 tbsp butter

1 8 oz. Package elbow
  macaroni

salt and pepper to
  taste

1 ½ cups shredded
  cheddar cheese

1 can drained
  mushrooms, (4oz.)

1 tsp. Basil

½ tsp oregano

Preheat oven to 350. Cook and drain macaroni. In a large skillet brown beef, remove and set aside. In the same skillet sautee onion in butter until onion is tender. Drain fat. In a large bowl combine beef, onion, spaghetti sauce, macaroni, 1 cup cheese, mushrooms and all other herbs. Spoon into an 11x7 baking dish and bake covered for 20 minutes. Sprinkle with ½ cup cheese in last 5 minutes of baking time.

Serves 4   35 minutes

Shopping List

Macaroni Beef Casserole

1 lb. ground beef
1 large yellow onion
1 package butter
1 8oz. box of elbow macaroni
1 bag shredded cheddar cheese
1 can mushrooms
Basil
Oregano

Beef and Cream Cheese Muffins

4 Bay's English
 Muffins, toasted

4 tbsp. cream cheese
 with chives

1 bottle steak sauce

4 tsp. White
 horseradish

6 oz. Thinly sliced
 roast beef

Spread muffin halves with cream cheese, then horseradish. Arrange roast beef on muffins and add steak sauce to taste.

Serves 4   20 Minutes

Shopping List

Beef and Cream Cheese Muffins

1 bag English Muffins
1 package cream cheese with chives
1 bottle steak sauce
1 bottle White Horseradish
6oz. thinly sliced roast beef

Steak Sandwich Supreme

1 can, 8 oz tomato sauce

¼ cup yellow mustard

½ cup water

1 tsp. onion salt

8 crusty rolls

3 tbsp. brown sugar

2 tbsp. Worcestershire sauce

¼ cup oil

1 boneless chuck steak, 2- 3 lbs

2 tbsp. soy sauce

Combine all ingredients in sauce pan and simmer 10 minutes. Grill or broil steak for 20 minutes turning twice. Slice steak into thin pieces and add to sauce. Let simmer for 10 minutes and serve over crusty rolls cut into half.

Serves 4

35 Minutes

Shopping List

Steak Sandwich Supreme

1 can (8oz.) tomato sauce
Yellow mustard
Onion salt
8 crusty rolls
Brown sugar
Worcestershire sauce
Cooking oil
1 boneless chuck steak, 2-3 lbs.
Soy sauce

Creamed Chipped Beef

6 tbsp. margarine

4 cups reconstituted non fat dry milk

1 can peas drained

6 tbsp flour

3 oz package dried beef

Melt margarine. Remove from heat. Stir in flour slowly. Gradually stir in milk. Add beef and peas and cook until sauce thickens. Serve over toast.

Serves 2   40 minutes

Shopping List

Creamed Chipped Beef

Margarine
2 cans reconstituted non-fat dry milk
1 can peas
Flour
3oz. package of dried beef
1 loaf bread

Pork and
Ham Recipes

Range Top Pork Chop Casserole

4 thin pork chops

1 tbsp soy sauce

1/2 cup water

1 medium sliced onion

1 box scalloped potatoes

½ tsp. each salt and pepper

1½ cup milk

Brown pork chops in large fry pan. Remove from pan. Open box of potatoes and arrange evenly over the bottom of fry pan. Add potato ingredients, water and milk and place the chops evenly over the potatoes. Add salt, pepper and soy sauce to top of chops. Add slices of onion on top of chops. Cover and simmer 25 minutes.

Serves 4   **40 minutes**

Shopping List

Range Top Pork Chop Casserole

4 thin pork chops
Soy sauce
1 medium yellow onion
1 box scalloped potatoes
Salt, Pepper
Milk

Sweet and Spicy Pork Chops with Rice

4 - 1" thick pork chops
½ cup apricot preserves
1 sliced onion

1 bag minute rice
¼ cup soy sauce
½ cup water

Brown chops in skillet. In baking dish, add rice and smooth out until rice is evenly distributed on the bottom of the dish. Add chops on top of rice. Add slices of onion and water. Combine apricots and soy sauce and spoon over chops. Cover in foil and bake in oven at 350 for 35 minutes.

Serves 4   45 minutes

Shopping List

Sweet and Spicy Pork Chops with Rice

4 thick pork chops (1")
Apricot preserves
1 yellow onion
Minute rice
Soy sauce

Mushroom and Rice Pork Chops

4 Medium to thin pork chops

1 bag minute rice

¼ cup onions cut into rings

1 can mushroom soup

½ tsp each salt and pepper

Brown chops on both sides and remove from skillet. Spray large baking pan with Pam and add rice, smoothing rice evenly in pan. Add chops, salt and pepper, onion and spoon soup over chops. Bake 30 minutes at 360.

Serves 4   40 minutes

Shopping List

Mushroom and Rice Pork Chops

4 medium pork chops
Minute rice
1 small yellow onion
1 can mushroom soup
Salt, Pepper

Ham and Spinach Pie

9" pie shell,
  unbaked

4 eggs

¾ cup milk

¼ tsp salt

1 ½ cups diced cooked
  ham

10 oz. chopped spinach

1 tbsp. minced onion

1/8 tsp pepper

Bake pie shell for 5 minutes in 375 degree preheated oven. Remove from oven. Mix all ingredients in bowl except ham. Add ingredients to shell, then spoon ham in evenly. Bake 25 to 30 minutes. (Add shredded cheddar cheese if desired 5 minutes before baking time has expired).

Serves 4   40 minutes

Shopping List

Ham and Spinach Pie

1 unbaked 9" pie shell
Eggs
Milk
Salt, Pepper
1 package thick ham slices
10 oz. chopped spinach
Minced onion

Monterey Ham and Cheese Pie

1 package refrigerated
crescent rolls

2 eggs beaten

½ lb. Monterey cheese,
cubed

1 cup shredded
cheddar cheese

½ cup chopped onion

¼ cup chopped
green pepper

½ cup shredded
mozzarella

2 cups cooked diced
ham

salt and pepper to taste

Line a 10" pie pan with ½ of the crescent rolls. Make sure that the rolls are pressed together. Mix all ingredients and pour into the pie pan. Arrange dough over the top making sure they overlap. Bake at 350 for 35 minutes or until a knife inserted in the middle comes out clean.

Serves 5   45 minutes

Shopping List

Monterey Ham and Cheese Pie

1 package refrigerated crescent rolls
1 block Monterey cheese
1 green pepper
1 Package thick ham slices
Eggs
1 bag shredded cheddar cheese
1 yellow onion
1 bag shredded Mozzarella cheese
Salt, Pepper

Italian Sausage Casserole

2 tbsp olive oil

1 jar meatless
    spaghetti sauce
    (26oz)

1 green pepper,
    thinly sliced

1/8 cup minced
    garlic

12 oz cooked drained
    rigatoni

2 cups shredded
    mozzarella

1 lb mild Italian sausage
    cut into 1" pieces

In a large skillet, heat oil and add garlic and peppers. Sauté until peppers are tender. Remove garlic and peppers and add sausage. Cook until brown. Drain off fat, combine vegetables, sausage, spaghetti sauce, pasta and 1 ½ cups of cheese. Spoon mixture into 3 quart casserole and bake at 350 for 30 minutes. Sprinkle on remaining cheese and bake 5 additional minutes.

Serves 6   45 minutes

Shopping List

Italian Sausage Casserole

Olive oil
1 jar meatless spaghetti sauce (26oz.)
1 green pepper
1 bag rigatoni
1 bag shredded Mozzarella cheese
1 lb Italian sausage (mild or spicy)
Minced garlic

Fish Recipes

Tuna or Salmon Noodle Casserole

1 can celery soup

½ cup sour cream

½ cup milk

1 can, drained and flaked tuna/ salmon

1 package shredded cheddar cheese

2 tbsp. pimiento

¼ tsp salt, pepper to taste

1 small can mushrooms

2 ½ cups cooked noodles

½ cup chopped celery

In 1 ½ quart casserole combine soup and sour cream and stir in milk. Add tuna or salmon, Pimiento, celery, mushrooms and noodles. Bake at 400 degrees for 30 minutes, top with cheese and bake an additional 5 minutes.

Serves 4   45 minutes

Shopping List

Tuna or salmon Noodle Casserole

1 can celery soup
Sour cream
Milk
1 can tuna or salmon
1 bag shredded cheddar cheese
Pimiento
Salt, Pepper
1 can mushrooms
1 bag thick noodles
1 stalk of celery

Whitefish Bake

1 ½ lb. white fish (any kind)

½ cup margarine or butter

2/3 cup milk

1 cup shredded cheddar cheese

1 can New England Clam chowder

1 cup chopped onion

2 cups cooked colored noodles, drained

Sauté onion in butter/ margarine, mix noodles in and place in baking dish. Place fish on top of noodles. Mix soup and milk and pour over fish. Bake covered for 30 minutes at 350. Remove cover and sprinkle with shredded cheese if desired, otherwise bake uncovered an additional 5 minutes.

Serves 5   45 minutes

Shopping List

Whitefish Bake

1 ½ lbs. white fish
Butter
Milk
1 can New England Clam Chowder
1 medium yellow onion
1 bag noodles
1 bag shredded cheddar cheese

Oven Fried Catfish

1 box of any fish coating
4 catfish fillets
1 box of minute rice (boil in a bag) or
   Rice A Roni

Follow directions on box to coat fish. Boil rice and follow directions on box. Pan fry fish when rice is cooked. Place fish on or next to rice on serving plate. Garnish with lemon wedges if desired.

Serves 2   40 minutes

Shopping List

Oven Fried Catfish

4 catfish fillets
1 lemon
1 box of Minute Rice or
Rice A Roni
1 box any fish coating

Soup Recipes

Autumn Soup

1 lb. ground beef

1 cup chopped onion

1 cup carrots, cut up

2 cups peeled and cubed potatoes

1 tsp bottled brown bouquet sauce

1 bay leaf

1 can whole tomatoes

4 cups water

1 cup diced celery

2 tsp. salt

¼ tsp pepper

1/8 tsp basil

Cook meat until brown in large sauce pan. Drain fat and onions with meat for 5 to 7 minutes. Stir in remaining ingredients except tomatoes in liquid. Heat to boiling, reduce heat, cover pan and simmer for 20 minutes. Stir in tomatoes with liquid and cover for 10 minutes or until potatoes are tender.

Serves 6   50 minutes

Shopping List

Autumn Soup

1 lb. ground beef
1 small yellow onion
Carrots
3 medium potatoes
1 bottle bouquet sauce
Bay leafs
1 can whole tomatoes
Celery
Salt, Pepper
Basil

Chicken / Turkey Rice Soup

2 cups chicken broth

2 tsp butter

1 tbsp corn starch with 2 tbsp water

¼ tsp. garlic powder

½ cup diced, cooked turkey or chicken

½ tsp Worcestershire Sauce

½ cup instant rice

salt and pepper to taste

Combine all ingredients except corn starch and water, in sauce pan. Heat slowly, until simmering. Combine corn starch and water in cup and mix completely. Slowly add to soup stirring continuously until thickened and bubbly.

Serves 2   30 minutes

Shopping List

Chicken or Turkey Rice Soup

1 can chicken broth
Butter
Corn Starch
Garlic powder
1 package diced cooked chicken or turkey
Worcestershire sauce
Instant rice
Salt, Pepper

End of the Day Vegetable Soup

½ package frozen mixed   1 cup water
   vegetables

1 small can mushrooms   4 cups milk

2 cans cream of potato soup

Combine vegetables and water, heat to boiling and
reduce heat to simmer for 6 minutes. Stir in soup and
milk slowly and stir several times. Serve when hot
completely.

Serves 4   35 minutes

Shopping List

End of the Day Vegetable Soup

1 package frozen mixed vegetables
1 can mushrooms
2 cans cream of potato soup
Milk

Vegetable Soup with Kielbasa

1 tbsp margarine

1 cup thinly sliced
   onion

8 oz. kielbasa sliced
   into sections

2 cans chicken broth

1 package frozen
   Japanese vegetables

½ cup Pastina (tiny
   star shaped pasta)

salt, pepper to taste

Melt margarine in large sauce pan, add onion and cook
5 minutes until tender. Add kielbasa and broth and bring
to boil. Add vegetables, Pastina and salt and pepper.
Cover and simmer 10 minutes.

Serves 4   40 minutes

Shopping List

Vegetable Soup with Kielbassa

Margarine
8 oz. kielbasa
1 package frozen Japanese vegetables
1 box Pastina (star shaped) pasta
1 small yellow onion
2 cans chicken broth
Salt, Pepper

Garden Vegetable Beef Soup

¾ lb. Beef cubes(small)   2 ¾ cups water

1 can beef broth   ½ cup chopped
    celery

1 medium carrot slices   1 small zucchini
    into ¼" slices   cut up

1 small onion   1 small tomato
    quartered   diced

1 ½ tsp leaf basil   ¼ tsp thyme leaf
    crumbled   crumbled

Brown beef cubes in fry pan and remove from heat. Combine water, broth and vegetables, heat to boiling. Add beef to soup. Simmer covered for 25 minutes or until vegetables are tender.

Serves 2   40 minutes

Shopping List

Garden Vegetable Beef Soup

¾ lb. package of beef cubes
1 can beef broth
Carrots
1 small yellow onion
Basil
Celery
1 small zucchini
1 small tomato
Thyme

Salads

Tuna, Egg, and Green Pea Salad

1 head lettuce	4 eggs hard boiled and sliced into qtrs.
2 cups mayonnaise	1 can peas, drained

Cut lettuce into small pieces, add egg, peas and mayonnaise. Mix well and refrigerate 35 minutes. Mix again before serving.

Serves 4   40 minutes

Shopping List

Tuna, Egg and Pea Salad

1 head of lettuce
Mayonnaise
Eggs
1 can peas

Mexican Steak Salad

1lb. any kind of steak

1 jar of mild Picante sauce

1 cup shredded cheddar cheese

1 cup sour cream

2 tomatoes cut into wedges

1 head of lettuce

1 cup crushed tortilla chips

Cut lettuce into small pieces and refrigerate. Broil or grill steak to liking and cut into thin 1" strips. Combine lettuce, steak, Picante sauce, cheese and tomatoes and mix well. Add crushed tortilla chips and serve chilled.

Serves 6   30 minutes

Shopping List

Mexican Steak Salad

1 lb. any kind of steak
Picante sauce
1 bag shredded cheddar cheese
Sour cream
2 tomatoes
1 head lettuce or 1 bag of lettuce
Tortilla chips

Green Beans Bacon and Potatoes

2 lbs fresh green beans
6 medium potatoes cooked
   and cubed
¼ cup diced onions

1 lb. bacon
1 small can
   mushrooms

Cut bacon into small strips ½ " long. Brown bacon and onions and pour off most of bacon drippings. Keep 1 tablespoon of bacon drippings. Wash and cut the green beans and combine green beans, potatoes, onion, mushrooms and bacon including bacon drippings in a 6 quart pot. Simmer on medium heat for 45 minutes.

Makes 4 servings

Shopping List

Green Beans, Bacon and Potatoes

2 lbs. fresh green beans
6 medium potatoes
1 small yellow onion
1 lb. bacon
1 small can mushrooms

Things That Go
With Beer

Spicy Pasta and Shrimp

½ lb. peeled medium frozen shrimp

¼ cup chopped green onion

1 tbsp Cajun seasoning

½ cup white wine

1/3 cup grated parmesan cheese

¼ cup chopped fresh parsley

2 tbsp butter

½ minced garlic clove

½ cup whipping cream

8 oz. Linguine, cooked

1 ½ tsp dry red pepper

Open bag of shrimp and run under cold water, drain and set aside. Melt butter in large skillet. Add green onion and garlic, sauté. Stir in Cajun seasoning and stir for one minute constantly. Stir in shrimp and whipping cream, reduce heat and simmer, stirring often for 3 minutes. Stir in wine and simmer for another 3 minutes. Add the remaining ingredients stirring constantly for another 5 minutes. Pour over pasta and mix well.

Serves 3   35 minutes

Shopping List

Spicy Pasta and Shrimp

1 bag frozen peeled and cooked shrimp
Green onion
1 packet of Cajun seasoning
White wine
1 can grated Parmesan cheese
Fresh parsley
Butter
Minced garlic
Whipping cream
1 bag Linguini
Dry red pepper

Stuffed Peppers

4 Green Peppers

1 medium onion
   chopped

1 package of instant
   rice

1 package of shredded
   sharp cheddar
   cheese

1 ½ lb. Ground beef

½ tsp salt

1 16 oz. Can of tomato
   sauce

Cut tops off peppers, remove seeds, put in large saucepan covered with water and boil until almost tender (5-7min). Brown beef, add salt, and onion in fry pan and drain fat. Boil rice for 3 minutes, rice will not be tender. Mix meat, onion, rice, cheese, and ½ can of tomato sauce. Add to peppers and spoon on remaining tomato sauce. Bake at 350 for 20 to 25 minutes.

Serves 4   50 minutes

Shopping List

Stuffed Peppers

4 large green peppers
1 medium yellow onion
Instant rice
1 bag shredded sharp cheddar cheese
1 ½ lb. ground beef
1 16oz. can tomato sauce
Salt

Beef and Tomato Casserole

1 lb. Ground beef

1 cup shredded
   cheddar cheese

2 cups cooked drained
   noodles

¼ cup water

½ cup chopped onion

1 can (10 3/4oz)
   tomato soup

1 ½ cup fresh frozen
   corn

1 can (8 oz) diced
   tomatoes

Brown beef and onion and drain fat. Add remaining ingredients except cheese and stir until well mixed. Add to a 1 ½ qt. casserole. Add cheese and bake at 350 for 30 minutes.

Serves 4   45 minutes

Shopping List

Beef and Tomato Casserole

1 lb. ground beef
1 bag shredded cheddar cheese
1 bag noodles
1 small yellow onion
1 can (10 3/4 oz) tomato soup
1 box frozen corn
1 can diced tomatoes

Beef Teriyaki

½ cup Soy Sauce

½ green and red pepper
cut into ½ inch by ¼
inch slices

1 package minute rice

1 cup water

1 package oriental
vegetables

1 small strip steak
sliced into 1inch
slices

1 small onion
chopped

Brown the steak in fry pan with soy sauce until brown on both sides. Add remaining ingredients and simmer 30 minutes. Add additional water if needed after 30 minutes.

Makes 4 servings   45 minutes

Shopping List

Beef Teriyaki

Soy sauce
1 green and 1 red pepper
1 small strip steak
Minute rice
1 package oriental vegetables
1 small yellow onion

Game Day Chili

1 can kidney beans
   and juice

1 ½ lb. ground beef

1 medium onion
   chopped

¼ tsp of chili powder

¼ tsp. Garlic salt

1 can chili beans

1 green pepper chopped

1 26 oz. can of tomato
   soup

1 can of diced tomatoes
   with garlic

1 package of dry onion
   soup

In a 5 quart pot, brown the ground beef allowing the beef to fry in medium chunks. Drain grease and add all other ingredients including the juice from the kidney beans. Simmer on medium heat for 45 minutes. Do not boil. Best when made the day before and reheated.

Makes 6 servings

Shopping List

Game Day Chile

1 can chili beans
1 can kidney beans
1 ½ lb. ground beef
1 yellow onion
1 green pepper
Chili powder
1 can of tomatoes with roasted garlic
1 package of dry onion soup
1 26 oz. tomato soup
Garlic salt

Mac and Cheese

2 cups of elbow
macaroni

1 cup of cubed
Velveeta cheese

½ cup of margarine

2 cups of shredded
cheddar cheese

1 ½ cups of milk

1 tsp. Salt

Cook and drain macaroni. In the same pot, combine milk, margarine and salt. Pour one half of the macaroni in a 2 qt. baking dish and add one half of both cheeses. Add the remainder of the macaroni and top with cheeses, spreading evenly. Bake at 350 for 15 minutes then stir. Bake an additional 10 to 15 minutes until cheese is golden brown.

Makes 4-5 servings

Shopping List

Mac and Cheese

1 box elbow macaroni
1 bag of shredded cheddar cheese
1 Velveeta cheese
Milk
Salt
Margarine

CPSIA information can be obtained at www.ICGtesting.com
Printed in the USA
BVOW081917250413

319150BV00004BA/310/A